Rise and Shine

Wake Up to Hot Breakfast Month - 40 Sweet and Savory Breakfast Recipes

By

Martha Stephenson

Copyright 2018 Martha Stephenson

License Notes

No part of this Book can be reproduced in any form or by any means including print, electronic, scanning or photocopying unless prior permission is granted by the author.

All ideas, suggestions and guidelines mentioned here are written for informative purposes. While the author has taken every possible step to ensure accuracy, all readers are advised to follow information at their own risk. The author cannot be held responsible for personal and/or commercial damages in case of misinterpreting and misunderstanding any part of this Book

Table of Contents

Introduction 6

Sweet 9

    Blueberry Croissant Breakfast Bake 10

    Caramelized Pecan Breakfast Casserole 13

    Carrot and Walnut Cake Pancakes 16

    Cherry Clafoutis 19

    Creamy Coconut Porridge with Raspberry Preserves 22

    Double Chocolate Waffles 24

    French Toast Bites 27

    Fruity Almond Breakfast Polenta 30

    Hot Breakfast Compote 32

    Icelandic Pancakes 34

    Maple and Molasses Sweet Potato Breakfast Bowl 37

    Nutty Berry Breakfast Quinoa 39

    PB&B Breakfast Pizza 42

    Roasted Sweet Potato Boats with Yogurt and Honey ... 45

Warm Applesauce Banana Muffins 48

Savory 50

Breakfast Bowl with Hummus and Fried Egg 51

Breakfast Linguine with Bacon 53

Croque Monsieur 57

Cube Steak and Eggs Breakfast 60

Easy Baked Bean Casserole 64

Easy Tostadas 67

Florentine Style Kippers with Eggs 70

Ful Medames - Egyptian-Style Breakfast Beans 73

Greek Breakfast Omelet 76

Mexican Hash Brown Breakfast Cupcakes 79

Savory French Toast Breakfast Bake 82

Smoked Mackerel Kedgeree 85

Smoked Trout with Mascarpone Scrambled Eggs 89

Southern Sausage Gravy 92

Spinach and Egg Frittata 95

Sweet and Savory 97

Cinnamon French Toast and Pancetta Casserole 98

Fennel Maple Bacon.. 101

Fried Banana Bacon Breakfast Sandwiches 103

Peach and Bacon Omelet... 106

Peaches and Cream Breakfast Cake with Cottage Cheese
.... 109

Pear and Bacon Grilled Cheese Sandwich 112

Pomegranate and Avocado Superfood Toast.............. 115

Raspberry Brie Grilled Cheese 117

Strawberry Chili Jam Breakfast Sandwich................. 119

Zucchini and Pineapple Bread 122

About the Author 126

Author's Afterthoughts.. 128

Introduction

Breakfast may very well be the most important meal of the day but did you know that breakfast foods vary wildly from country to country?

Greeks grab a black coffee and a cheese pie while in France, the morning meal is a sweet pastry washed down with a strong coffee.

While the Brits love nothing more than a full English with bacon, eggs, sausage, and beans, one thing is for sure Americans love breakfast!

In fact, the Constitution states that the official American breakfast consists of eggs, bacon, toast, orange juice and coffee.

Unfortunately, most people settle for cold cereal, yogurt or at best toast, with pancakes and waffles reserved for the weekend only.

February is Hot Breakfast Month so why not spoil yourself with a hot, home-cooked breakfast every morning.

Wake up to our 40 sweet and savory breakfast recipes including:

- Smoked Mackerel Kedgeree
- Greek Breakfast Omelet
- Spinach and Egg Frittata
- French Toasts Bites
- Icelandic Pancakes
- Roasted Sweet Potato Boats with Yogurt and Honey

We guarantee once you tasted our very best hot breakfast recipes you'll never reach for the cereal again!

Sweet

Blueberry Croissant Breakfast Bake

Quinoa is a tasty and versatile little grain packed with fiber and antioxidants; it's also gluten-free!

Portions: 8-10

Prep Time: 10mins

Cooking Time: 35mins

Total Time: 50mins

Ingredients:

- Nonstick spray
- 6 large croissants* (cubed)
- 8 medium eggs (lightly beaten)
- 2 tsp pure vanilla essence
- 1 tsp ground cinnamon
- 2 ripe large bananas (mashed)
- 1 cup whole milk
- ¼ cup light brown sugar
- 1 cup blueberries

Directions:

1. Preheat the main oven to 375 degrees F. Spritz a rectangular baking dish with nonstick spray.

2. Arrange the cubed croissants in the base of the baking dish.

3. In a jug, whisk together the eggs, vanilla essence, cinnamon, mashed bananas, and whole milk.

4. Pour the liquid over the croissants and press down on them to ensure they soak up as much of the liquid as possible.

5. Sprinkle with brown sugar and finish by scattering the blueberries over the top.

6. Place in the oven and bake for just over half an hour, until set.

7. Allow to sit for 5-7 minutes at room temperature before slicing and serving.

*Preferably one day old.

Caramelized Pecan Breakfast Casserole

This utterly scrumptious breakfast casserole is the ultimate weekend treat. Your little ones will be begging you to make it every day of the week!

Portions: 8-10

Prep Time: 15mins

Cooking Time: 40mins

Total Time: 8hours 55mins

Ingredients:

- Nonstick spray

Bake:

- 6 plain ring donuts (chopped)
- 7 medium eggs
- 1¼ cups whole milk
- 1 tsp vanilla essence
- Pinch kosher salt

Caramel:

- 1½ cups light brown sugar
- ⅓ cup corn syrup
- 6 tbsp. salted butter
- ½ tsp kosher salt
- ½ cup heavy cream
- ½ cup raw pecans (chopped)

Directions:

1. Spritz a 3-quart baking dish with nonstick spray.

2. Place the chopped donuts in the base of the dish.

3. In a jug, whisk together the eggs, whole milk, vanilla, and kosher salt. Pour the mixture over the croissants in the dish. Cover with aluminum foil and chill overnight.

4. The following day preheat the main oven to 350 degrees F and prepare the caramel. In a saucepan over moderate heat, melt together the brown sugar, corn syrup, salted butter, and kosher salt while stirring. Take off the heat.

5. Stir in half of the heavy cream until combined. Add the remaining cream, and stir. Allow to cool a little before pouring over the chilled donut mixture.

6. Scatter with the chopped pecans.

7. Bake in the oven for approximately 25-30 minutes, or until set.

8. Allow to cool a little before slicing and serving warm.

Carrot and Walnut Cake Pancakes

Sweet aromatic pancakes spiced with cinnamon, nutmeg, and ginger and studded with plump golden raisins will get the whole family out of bed.

Portions: 4

Prep Time: 10mins

Cooking Time: 20mins

Total Time: 30mins

Ingredients:

- 8 ounces all-purpose flour
- ½ tsp bicarb of soda
- 1 tsp baking powder
- ½ tsp kosher salt
- ½ tsp fresh nutmeg (grated)
- ½ tsp cinnamon
- ⅛ tsp powdered ginger
- 2 tbsp. walnuts (chopped)
- 2 tbsp. golden sultanas
- 1 egg
- 2 tbsp. light brown sugar
- 1 cup buttermilk
- 1 tsp vanilla essence
- ¾ pound whole carrots (peeled, grated)
- 3 tbsp. salted butter
- Maple syrup (for serving)

Directions:

1. Whisk together the flour, bicarb of soda, baking powder, kosher salt, spices, walnuts, and golden sultanas.

2. In a jug, beat together the egg, light brown sugar, buttermilk, and vanilla essence until combined. Pour into the dry flour mixture and stir well until incorporated. Fold in the grated carrot until evenly distributed. Set aside to rest for 5-6 minutes.

3. In a skillet over moderate heat, melt a little of the butter. Spoon in two tablespoons of batter at a time and cook for 2 minutes each side. Repeat with the remaining butter and batter.

4. Serve the pancakes with lashing of maple syrup.

Cherry Clafoutis

Clafoutis is a super fluffy and light breakfast sponge studded with plump, juicy cherries, which burst in the mouth releasing sweet fruity flavor. These individual-sized portions make serving super easy.

Portions: 4

Prep Time: 10mins

Cooking Time: 20mins

Total Time: 30mins

Ingredients:

- ¼ cup all-purpose flour
- 1½ tbsp. sugar
- Pinch kosher salt
- 1 medium egg
- ½ cup heavy cream
- ¼ tsp vanilla essence
- 1 tbsp. unsalted butter (melted)
- Fresh sweet cherries (pitted)

Directions:

1. Preheat the main oven to 425 degrees F. Set aside 4 ramekins.

2. Sift together the flour, sugar, and salt together into a bowl.

3. Whisk together the egg, cream, vanilla, and melted butter. Mix the cream mixture into the flour mixture, a little at a time, until incorporated.

4. Place 4-5 cherries in the bottom of each ramekin. Pour the batter equally over the top of each one.

5. Place the ramekins in the oven for approximately 20 minutes, and bake until set. Serve hot.

Creamy Coconut Porridge with Raspberry Preserves

A thick and creamy bowl of hot coconutty porridge is just what the doctor ordered, especially on those cold winter mornings.

Portions: 1-2

Prep Time: 5mins

Cooking Time: 7mins

Total Time: 12mins

Ingredients:

- ½ cup old-fashioned porridge oats
- 2 tbsp. canned coconut milk
- Pinch coconut sugar
- 1 cup water
- 2 tbsp. desiccated coconut
- Raspberry preserves

Directions:

1. In a saucepan over low heat, add the oats, coconut milk, coconut sugar, and water. Stir well and cook for 5-6 minutes,

2. Stir in the desiccated coconut. Spoon into (a) bowl(s).

3. Top with a spoonful of raspberry preserves and enjoy.

Double Chocolate Waffles

Double chocolate waffles make a scrummy, hot breakfast treat, especially when served with fresh whip cream and berries.

Portions: 4

Prep Time: 10mins

Cooking Time: 20mins

Total Time: 35mins

Ingredients:

- 1½ cups all-purpose flour
- 3 tbsp. granulated sugar
- ½ cup sweetened cocoa powder
- ½ tsp bicarb of soda
- 1 tsp baking powder
- 1 tsp kosher salt
- 3 eggs (lightly beaten)
- 4 tbsp. salted butter (melted, cooled)
- 1 tsp vanilla essence
- 2 cups buttermilk
- ¾ cup mini milk choc chips
- Nonstick spray
- Whip cream (for topping)
- Fresh berries (for topping)

Directions:

1. Preheat your waffle iron.

2. Combine the all-purpose flour, granulated sugar, sweetened cocoa powder, bicarb of soda, baking powder, and kosher salt in a large mixing bowl.

3. In a jug, whisk together the egg, melted butter, vanilla essence, and buttermilk. Pour into the dry flour mixture a little at a time, while stirring, until combined. Fold in the mini choc chips. Allow the batter to rest for several minutes.

4. Spritz your waffle iron with nonstick cooking spray.

5. Cook the batter in the waffle iron according to the manufacturer's directions.

6. Serve in batches with whip cream and fresh fruit.

French Toast Bites

Cubes of French toast are soaked in cinnamon-spiced vanilla milk and fried in butter for a heavenly breakfast that smells as good as it tastes.

Portions: 4

Prep Time: 10mins

Cooking Time: 7mins

Total Time: 17mins

Ingredients:

- 3 medium eggs
- ½ cup skim milk
- 1 tsp vanilla essence
- ½ tsp cinnamon
- ½ loaf firm French bread* (crusts removed, cut into 1" cubed)
- Butter (for cooking)
- Powdered sugar (for dusting)

Directions:

1. Beat together the eggs, skim milk, vanilla essence, and cinnamon in a shallow bowl. Add the cubed bread and toss to saturate.

2. Melt a little butter in a skillet over moderately high heat.

3. Use a slotted spoon to lift the soaked bread cubes from the liquid and set them in the skillet.

4. Cook, while tossing, for 5-6 minutes, or until golden.

5. Transfer to a serving plate and dust with powdered sugar.

6. Serve immediately.

*Preferably one day old.

Fruity Almond Breakfast Polenta

polenta drizzled with honey and topped with chopped fruit and almonds is a delicious and satisfying breakfast that will set you and your family up for the day.

Portions: 4

Prep Time: 10mins

Cooking Time: 35mins

Total Time: 45mins

Ingredients:

- 4 cups water
- ½ tsp kosher salt
- 1 cup polenta (coarse variety, not quick cooking)
- ½ cup toasted slivered almonds
- ½ cup mixed dried fruit (chopped)
- Organic honey

Directions:

1. Bring the water to a boil in a large saucepan. Add the salt and polenta. Stir continuously for 5 minutes before turning the heat down. Simmer for just over 30 minutes.

2. Spoon into bowls; evenly scatter over the almonds and fruit. Finish with a drizzle of honey.

Hot Breakfast Compote

You can prepare this scrummy fruity compote in just 15 minutes. Just top with a fluffy dollop of whip cream or yogurt and dig right in!

Portions: 2-3

Prep Time: 5mins

Cooking Time: 6mins

Total Time: 17mins

Ingredients:

- 5⅓ ounces mixed dried fruits
- 1 cup boiling water
- ¼ cup organic apple juice
- Ground cinnamon
- ½ cup plain full-fat yogurt or whip cream

Directions:

1. In a microwave-safe bowl, add the dried fruits to the boiling water. Cook on high heat for 5-6 minutes.

2. Remove from the microwave and stir in the apple juice and cinnamon. Set to one side for 5-6 minutes.

3. Spoon into bowls and top each portion with a spoonful of yogurt or whip cream.

4. Enjoy while warm.

Icelandic Pancakes

Icelanders like their pancakes thin, sweet, and delicious with a light crispiness. They typically serve them rolled up like cigars with a dollop of creamy yogurt, organic preserves, and seasonal fruit.

Portions: 4-5

Prep Time: 10mins

Cooking Time: 15mins

Total Time: 25mins

Ingredients:

- 1½ cups plain flour
- ½ tsp bicarb of soda
- ½ tsp kosher salt
- 2 tbsp. granulated sugar
- 3 medium eggs
- 3 cups whole milk
- ¼ cup salted butter (melted)
- Yogurt, organic fruit preserves, seasonal fruit (to serve)

Directions:

1. Sift together the flour, bicarb of soda, kosher salt, and sugar. Beat in the eggs, milk, and melted butter until combined.

2. Cook the batter in a non-stick frying pan, in batches, until golden.

3. When cooked, turn out of the pan and roll up into a cigar shape.

4. Serve the warm pancakes with yogurt, preserves, and fresh fruit.

Maple and Molasses Sweet Potato Breakfast Bowl

Adding a spoonful of molasses gives this hearty sweet potato breakfast bowl a dark rich caramel flavor.

Portions: 2

Prep Time: 5mins

Cooking Time: 10mins

Total Time: 15mins

Ingredients:

- ¾ cup pureed sweet potato
- 1 tsp molasses
- 2 tbsp. pure maple syrup
- ⅓ cup old-fashioned oats
- 1 cup vanilla flavor almond milk
- 1 tsp vanilla essence
- ½ tsp ground cinnamon

Directions:

1. In a medium saucepan, combine the sweet potato puree, molasses, maple syrup, oats, almond milk, vanilla, and cinnamon. Stir well and cook over a moderate heat for approximately 10 minutes, or until the mixture is nice and thick.

2. Spoon into bowls and enjoy immediately.

Nutty Berry Breakfast Quinoa

Quinoa is a tasty and versatile little grain packed with fiber and antioxidants; it's also gluten-free which makes it a great hot breakfast choice.

Portions: 1

Prep Time: 10mins

Cooking Time: 20mins

Total Time: 30mins

Ingredients:

- 2⅔ ounces quinoa
- 7 ounces water
- 3½ ounces semi skim milk
- ½ tsp cinnamon
- 2 tbsp. organic honey
- 1¾ ounces fresh raspberries
- 1 tbsp. roasted hazelnuts (chopped)
- 1 tbsp. toasted slivered almonds

Directions:

1. Rinse the quinoa under hot running water using a fine-mesh nylon sieve.

2. Add the quinoa to a deep pot along with 7 ounces of water and bring to a boil before reducing to a simmer. Cook for 15 minutes, drain.

3. In the meantime, warm together the milk, cinnamon, and honey using a microwave. Stir well to combine.

4. Transfer the cooked quinoa to a bowl, pour over the warmed milk and scatter over the raspberries and nuts.

PB&B Breakfast Pizza

We have all heard of PB&J, but have you heard of PB&B!? Peanut butter and banana is a marriage made in heaven and the ideal topping for a sweet, breakfast pizza.

Portions: 1

Prep Time: 10mins

Cooking Time: 8mins

Total Time: 18mins

Ingredients:

Pizza base:

- ¼ cup organic chickpea flour
- ¼ cup vanilla flavor almond milk
- 2 tsp maple syrup
- ½ tsp cinnamon
- ½ tsp pure vanilla essence
- Nonstick spray

Topping:

- 1½ tbsp. smooth peanut butter
- 1 large banana (peeled, sliced)
- Choc chips

Directions:

1. Beat together the flour, milk, maple syrup, cinnamon, and vanilla until you have a smooth batter.

2. Spritz a skillet with nonstick spray.

3. Pour the batter into the skillet and cook for 5 minutes before flipping. Cook for another 2-3 minutes.

4. Turn the crust out onto a plate. Spread over the peanut butter and scatter over the banana and choc chips.

5. Enjoy!

Roasted Sweet Potato Boats with Yogurt and Honey

A nutritious and hearty breakfast that will keep you full 'til lunch. Change up your toppings for a versatile weekday hot breakfast.

Portions: 2-4

Prep Time: 10mins

Cooking Time: 35mins

Total Time: 45mins

Ingredients:

- 2 medium-sized sweet potatoes (washed, halved lengthwise)
- 1 tbsp. virgin olive oil
- 1 tbsp. organic honey
- Cinnamon
- 8 ounces plain full-fat yogurt
- 1 medium ripe banana (peeled, sliced)
- 1 tbsp. cacao nibs

Directions:

1. Preheat the main oven to 400 degrees F. Cover a baking tray with aluminum foil.

2. Rub the sweet potato halves with olive oil and arrange flat-side facing down on the baking tray.

3. Place in the oven and bake for 25 minutes.

4. Remove the baking tray from the oven, flip the potatoes and drizzle with honey. Sprinkle with a pinch of cinnamon. Cook for another 5-10 minutes.

5. Arrange the sweet potato halves on plates. Top each half with a dollop of yogurt. Scatter with sliced banana and cacao nibs.

6. Enjoy!

Warm Applesauce Banana Muffins

There are few things better in life than starting the day with a warm muffin slathered with butter. If you're short on time, make ahead and microwave your muffins until warm before enjoying, for a super quick grab and go breakfast treat.

Portions: 12

Prep Time: 10mins

Cooking Time: 25mins

Total Time: 35mins

Ingredients:

- 2 ripe large bananas (peeled, chopped)
- ½ cup granulated sugar
- ¼ cup organic applesauce
- 1 cup wholewheat flour
- ½ tsp bicarb of soda
- ½ tbsp. baking powder
- ½ tsp kosher salt
- 1 tsp vanilla essence
- 1 medium egg
- Salted butter (for serving)

Directions:

1. Preheat the main oven to 350 degrees F.

2. In a bowl, mash together the banana and sugar, until combined. Beat in the applesauce, flour, bicarb of soda, baking powder, salt, vanilla essence, and egg.

3. Pour the batter into a muffin tin. Place in the oven and bake for approximately 20 minutes.

4. Serve while still very warm with plenty of butter.

Savory

Breakfast Bowl with Hummus and Fried Egg

Work those veggies into the most important meal of the day.

Servings: 1

Prep Time: 5mins

Cooking Time: 8mins

Total Time: 13mins

Ingredients:

- 1 large egg
- 4 broccoli florets
- 1 cup rice (cooked)
- 2 tbsp. hummus
- Pinch salt
- Dash of pepper
- Sriracha (to taste)
- 1 tsp sesame seeds

Directions:

1. First, in a frying pan, fry the egg, leaving the yolk runny, this will give you additional "sauce" for the breakfast bowl.

2. In the meantime, and while the egg is frying, steam the broccoli until fork tender.

3. On high power, microwave the cooked rice on high for 60 seconds, or until hot.

4. Transfer the rice to a breakfast bowl, top with the broccoli, followed by the hummus, and a fried egg. Season to taste.

5. Drizzle with sriracha and scatter with sesame seeds.

Breakfast Linguine with Bacon

Maybe more breakfast than brunch but whatever time you wake up this is an ideal way to start the day.

Servings: 4-6

Prep Time: 10mins

Cooking Time: 30mins

Total Time: 40mins

Ingredients:

- 1 pound linguine
- 2-3 tbsp. salt
- 3 tbsp. extra virgin olive oil
- ½ pound baby new potatoes (quartered)
- Salt and black pepper (to season)
- 1 medium yellow onion (peeled, diced)
- ½ red bell pepper (diced)
- ½ green bell pepper (diced)
- 1 tbsp. fresh thyme (minced)
- 1 tbsp. unsalted butter
- 4 medium eggs + 2 egg whites (lightly beaten)
- ⅔ cup Cheddar cheese (grated)
- ½ pound bacon (cooked, crumbled)

Directions:

1. Fill a large saucepan with water, and over moderate to high heat, bring to boil.

2. As soon as the water boils, add the pasta, together with 2-3 tablespoons of salt.

3. Cook the linguine, while agitating, until al dente, this will take between 7-9 minutes. Drain and toss with a little oil. Set to one side.

4. Add more olive oil to a large skillet and place over a moderate heat.

5. Add the baby new potatoes to the skillet and season with salt and black pepper. Sauté the potatoes for 4-5 minutes, and then add the diced onion, along with the red bell peppers, the green bell peppers, and minced thyme. Season while stirring.

6. Continue cooking, for 6-8 minutes, or until veggies are fork tender.

7. Transfer the mixture to a bowl and set to one side.

8. Return the pan to the stovetop and over moderate heat add the unsalted butter.

9. Add the beaten eggs and whites to the pan and scramble gently for a couple of minutes.

10. Next, add the Cheddar cheese to the pan and stir. The mixture should be a little runny.

11. Transfer the cooked linguine and potato mixture to the pan and toss until incorporated, and when the eggs are sufficiently cooked, season.

12. Scatter the crumbled bacon over the linguine and serve hot.

Croque Monsieur

The dish originated in cafés and bars throughout France as a quick snack, but this dish makes an ideal breakfast.

Servings: 1

Prep Time: 7mins

Cooking Time: 8mins

Total Time: 15mins

Ingredients:

- 2 tbsp. butter
- 1 tbsp. flour
- ¾ cup whole milk
- Salt
- Dash of black pepper
- 2 pinches nutmeg (fresh, divided)
- 1 large egg
- ¼ tsp cinnamon
- 2 thick slices of white bread
- 1 slice ham steak
- ¼ cup Gruyere cheese (shredded)

Directions:

1. For the béchamel sauce: Using a small pan over moderate heat, melt 1 tablespoon of butter.

2. Add the flour and mix until combined, until a pale brown gravy begins to form.

3. Slowly, and gradually whisk in the whole milk, seasoning with the salt, black pepper and a pinch of nutmeg.

4. Reduce to low heat, and put to one side.

5. In a mixing bowl, whisk the egg and add a pinch of both nutmeg and cinnamon.

6. In a frying pan, melt half a tablespoon of butter.

7. Dip each of the 2 slices of white bread into the egg mixture and fry only one side of each slice until golden, set to one side.

8. Next, heat the slice of ham.

9. Assemble the sandwich: Place the cooked side of the white bread facing inwards. Layer the slice of ham, followed by the béchamel and then the cheese.

10. Add the remaining butter to the pan and continue to cook each sandwich, until each side is golden.

11. Serve while hot.

Cube Steak and Eggs Breakfast

A low-carb substantial keto breakfast which is also suitable for Atkins Induction.

Servings: 2

Prep Time: 10mins

Cooking Time: 10mins

Total Time: 20mis

Ingredients:

- 8 ounces asparagus (trimmed)
- Salt and freshly ground black pepper
- 8 ounces cube steak
- 2 tbsp. butter (divided)
- 4 large eggs
- 2 ounces Cheddar cheese

Directions:

1. Place the asparagus in a microwave-safe bowl. Add one tablespoon of cold water to the bowl and securely cover with a sheet of plastic wrap. Put to one side.

2. Next, season both sides of the steak.

3. Over moderate heat, heat a skillet. When hot, add half of the butter, swirling to coat the bottom of the skillet. Add the steak and cook for between 3-5 minutes, depending on your preferred doneness. When cooked, remove the steaks to a serving plate, tented with aluminum foil.

4. In the meantime, prepare the eggs. While the steak cooks, place a frying pan over moderate heat.

5. Crack the eggs into a medium-sized mixing bowl and sprinkle in the Cheddar cheese and using a fork, mix to combine.

6. As soon as the pan is sufficiently hot, add the remaining butter and swirl to coat.

7. Add the egg mixture and allow to cook for a few moments to allow it to cook on the bottom, using a rubber kitchen utensil, gently scraping the cooked egg towards the middle of the pan.

8. Using a spatula, break up the middle and turn the heat off. Every 30-40 seconds, gently push the cooked egg to the middle of the pan. Continue to break-up and fold the mixture. You should achieve a custard-like consistency.

9. While the eggs are cooking, place the microwave bowl containing the asparagus in the microwave and cook for 2 minutes. Allow to rest in the microwave until the eggs are cooked.

10. To serve, arrange the cooked cube steak on two dinner plates, divide the cooked asparagus between the steaks, and season. Arrange the cheesy eggs on top of the asparagus and season to taste.

Easy Baked Bean Casserole

Tired of toast? Then this satisfying breakfast is sure to keep those hunger pangs at bay.

Servings: 6-8

Prep Time: 10mins

Cooking Time: 1hour 30mins

Total Time: 1hour 40mins

Ingredients:

- 4 slices bacon
- ½ cup sweet onion (peeled, chopped)
- 3 (16 ounce) canned pork and beans in tomato sauce
- 3 tbsp. brown sugar
- 3 tbsp. ketchup
- 1½ tbsp. Worcestershire sauce
- 1½ tbsp. mustard

Directions:

1. In a frying pan, fry the bacon until crispy and set to one side on a kitchen paper towel lined plate, while reserving the bacon fat.

2. Preheat the main oven to 375 degrees F.

3. Cook the chopped onion in 2 tbsp. of bacon drippings, until the onions are translucent.

4. In a large mixing bowl, combine the pork and beans, with the sautéed onions and brown sugar, ketchup, Worcestershire sauce and mustard.

5. Pour the mixture into an 11x7" casserole dish and bake in the oven for 1½ hours.

6. Remove the dish from the oven and stir well to incorporate. Lay the bacon slices on top of the casserole and allow to rest for 2-3 minutes before serving.

Easy Tostadas

Tostada is the Spanish word for 'toasted,' and this makes a fabulous and filling meal.

Servings: 6

Prep Time: 10mins

Cooking Time: 7mins

Total Time: 17mins

Ingredients:

- 6 tostada shells
- 1 can (16 ounce) refried beans
- 6 medium eggs
- ¼ cup queso fresco (crumbled)
- 1 avocado (peeled, pitted, sliced)
- Salt and black pepper
- Cilantro
- Hot sauce

Directions:

1. Preheat the main oven to 325 degrees F.

2. In a single layer arrange each of the tostada shells on a baking tray and bake until crisp, this will take around 5-7 minutes.

3. In the meantime, put the refried beans into a saucepan and heat over moderate heat until sufficiently warmed through.

4. Cook the eggs to your preference.

5. Next, assemble the tostadas: Evenly divide the beans between the six shells, spreading evenly.

6. Top each shell with crumbled queso fresco, followed by avocado slices.

7. Place a cooked egg on top of each tostada and season with salt and black pepper.

8. Top with cilantro and hot sauce.

Florentine Style Kippers with Eggs

Spoil yourself with this hotel style breakfast.

Servings: 2

Prep Time: 6mins

Cooking Time: 12mins

Total Time: 18mins

Ingredients:

- 2 large eggs
- 2 smoked kippers
- 1 (8 ounce) bag baby leaf spinach
- Salt and black pepper
- Lemon wedges (to serve)
- Crusty bread (to serve)

Directions:

1. Fill a large frying pan with boiling water, and over high heat, bring to simmer.

2. Turn the heat down, and using a spoon quickly swirl the water. One at a time, drop each of the eggs into the swirling water and poach for 2-3 minutes or until the egg whites are just set, but the yolks remain runny.

3. Using a slotted spoon, remove the poached eggs from the pan and place on a kitchen paper lined plate to drain.

4. Add the two kippers to the simmering water to 2 minutes, or until heated through.

5. Transfer the kippers to kitchen paper to drain.

6. In the meantime, pierce the bag of spinach 2-3 times, and on high heat, microwave for a couple of minutes, until the spinach is just wilted.

7. Tip the spinach into a bowl, and season well with salt and black pepper.

8. Divide the seasoned spinach between two dinner plates.

9. Arrange the kippers on top of the spinach and top each kipper with a poached egg.

10. Serve with a wedge of lemon and crusty bread.

Ful Medames - Egyptian-Style Breakfast Beans

Ful Medames translates as 'stewed dried beans', which is a staple breakfast dish in Egypt.

Servings: 2

Prep Time: 10mins

Cooking Time: 20mins

Total Time: 30mins

Ingredients:

- 1 (15 ounce) canned fava beans (drained, rinsed)
- 1½ tbsp. virgin olive oil
- 1 medium onion (peeled, finely chopped)
- 1 large tomato (finely chopped)
- 1 tsp ground cumin
- 1-2 tbsp. freshly squeezed lemon juice
- Salt and pepper
- ¼ cup fresh parsley (chopped)
- Grilled flatbread (warmed)
- 2 medium eggs
- ¼ cup fresh parsley (chopped)
- Olive oil

Directions:

1. Add the rinsed beans to a medium-sized saucepan, bring to boil, and simmer for 5-6 minutes, using a fork to break them up.

2. Add the olive oil, and stir to combine, along with the chopped onion, chopped tomato, cumin, freshly squeezed lemon juice, salt, pepper and the majority of the chopped parsley. Continue to cook for another 5 minutes.

3. In the meantime, place the flatbread on the grill.

4. In a frying pan, fry the eggs in a drop of olive oil, making sure that the eggs remain runny.

5. Serve the beans alongside the fried eggs and warmed flatbread.

Greek Breakfast Omelet

For the majority of Greeks breakfast consists of a cup of strong black coffee, but when there is time to sit and chill, then this feta filled omelet is a welcome change.

Servings: 2

Prep Time: 10mins

Cooking Time: 8mins

Total Time: 18mins

Ingredients:

- 6 medium eggs (whisked)
- ¼ whole cup milk
- 1 tbsp. butter
- 1 tbsp. Greek extra virgin olive oil
- 1 cup spinach (lightly packed)
- 2 cloves garlic (peeled, minced)
- ¼ cup roasted red peppers (coarsely chopped)
- ¼ cup marinated artichoke hearts (roughly chopped)
- ½ tsp dried oregano
- ½ tsp dried basil
- ¼ tsp salt
- ¼ tsp black pepper
- ¼ cup cherry tomatoes (halved)
- ¼ cup kalamata olives (sliced)
- 2 tbsp. Greek feta cheese (crumbled)

Directions:

1. In a mixing bowl, whisk the eggs together with the whole milk, and put to one side.

2. In a large frying pan over moderate heat, heat the butter with the olive oil.

3. When hot, add the spinach along with the garlic and fry for 30-40 seconds, or until the spinach begins to wilt.

4. Next, add the chopped peppers, artichokes, oregano, basil, and seasoning. Fry for a couple of minutes, or until the vegetables soften. Remove the mixture from the pan and put to one side.

5. Add the egg-milk mixture to the pan and allow to rest for 40 seconds. Next, to only half of the omelet, add the spinach mixture, along with the cherry tomato halves, kalamata olives, and crumbled feta.

6. Cook for 3-5 minutes, or until the eggs are sufficiently cooked through. Fold the omelet over to cover the toppings and slide onto a plate.

7. Season with salt and pepper and serve.

Mexican Hash Brown Breakfast Cupcakes

Cupcakes go south of the border with this spicy and flavorful morning meal.

Servings: 6

Prep Time: 15mins

Cook Time: 30mins

Total Time: 50mins

Ingredients

- Nonstick spray
- 1 box (5.2 ounce) hash brown potatoes
- 1 small red onion (peeled, diced)
- 1 can (4½ ounce) can green chilies (chopped)
- ½ cup Cheddar cheese (shredded)
- 2 medium eggs (lightly beaten)
- 1 medium avocado (peeled, pitted, sliced)
- 1 cup sour cream
- Fresh cilantro leaves

Directions:

1. Preheat the main oven to 375 degrees F. Lightly mist a 12-cup muffin tray with nonstick cooking spray.

2. Prepare the hash brown potatoes according to the manufacturer's instructions, adding water and salt as directed but omitting any margarine. When cooked, transfer to a bowl.

3. Using the same skillet, over moderate heat, cook the diced onion until softened, while occasionally stirring.

4. Add the green chilies and Cheddar cheese along with the potatoes and stir in the beaten eggs.

5. Evenly divide the mixture between the muffin cups, to around 70% full, making sure to push the mixture down into the muffin cups.

6. Bake in the oven for between 25-30 minutes or until the muffin tops are crispy and golden. Allow to cool for 4-5 minutes.

7. Serve with sliced avocado, sour cream, and fresh cilantro leaves.

Savory French Toast Breakfast Bake

This bake in the oven casserole is perfect for a family breakfast get-together.

Servings: 4

Prep Time: 10mins

Cooking Time: 45mins

Total Time: 55mins

Ingredients:

- 1 tbsp. butter (softened)
- 4 slices French bread
- 5 slices of bacon (cooked, crumbled)
- 2 green onions (sliced)
- 4 white mushrooms (sliced)
- 1 cup Swiss cheese (shredded)
- 6 medium eggs
- 1½ cups milk
- 1½ tsp Dijon mustard
- 2 tbsp. fresh parsley (minced)
- Salt and black pepper (to season)

Directions:

1. Preheat the main oven to 350 degrees F.

2. Lightly grease an 8" square baking dish with the butter.

3. Arrange the slices of French bread in the bottom of the dish.

4. Scatter the crumbled bacon, along with the sliced onions, mushrooms and Swiss cheese on the top of the French bread.

5. In a mixing bowl, add the eggs, together with the milk, Dijon mustard, minced parsley, salt and black pepper and using a fork, beat until incorporated. When combined, pour the mixture over the top of the shredded Swiss cheese and using a fork press down to allow the mixture to absorb.

6. Bake in the preheated oven for 40-45 minutes, until the eggs are thoroughly set.

Smoked Mackerel Kedgeree

Although kedgeree was primarily enjoyed in Victorian Britain, it is in fact of Indian origin hence the inclusion of tikka paste.

Servings: 4

Prep Time: 15mins

Cooking Time: 25mins

Total Time: 40mins

Ingredients:

- 1 medium red onion (peeled, diced)
- 9 ounces mushrooms (halved)
- Olive oil
- 2 tsp medium curry powder
- 1 tsp ground cumin
- ½ tsp ground coriander
- 10 ounces rice
- 1 cup dairy-free milk
- 1 cup water
- 7 ounces green beans (cut into quarters)
- 12 ounces boneless smoked mackerel
- 10 cherry tomatoes (halved)
- ½ tsp turmeric
- 6 tbsp. tikka paste
- 4 medium eggs
- Handful fresh parsley (chopped)

Directions:

1. Add the onions and mushrooms to a large pan or wok over moderate heat, add a drop of olive oil and fry for 4-5 minutes until softened.

2. Add the curry powder to the pan, along with the cumin and coriander and mix well to combine, for a couple of minutes. Remove the pan from the heat and set to one side.

3. Cook the rice in 1 cup each of milk and water over moderate heat, for 15 minutes.

4. In the meantime, while the rice is cooking add the green beans to a microwave safe bowl, and on high heat, cook in the microwave for 4 minutes.

5. Next, remove the skin from the mackerel and break the fish into chunks.

6. Once the rice is cooked, drain and rinse in boiling water, this will remove any starch.

7. Add the eggs to a medium-sized saucepan of boiling water over moderate heat and cook for 6-7 minutes.

8. As the eggs cook, add the fish, tomatoes and green beans to the pan and place back on the stove top on moderate heat. Add the turmeric, mix well to combine and cook for 2-3 minutes.

9. Next, add the rice together with the tikka paste and stir well to incorporate. Remove the pan from the heat.

10. As soon as the eggs are ready, remove them from the water, and peel.

11. Cut each egg into quarters and place on top of the kedgeree.

12. Sprinkle with chopped parsley.

Smoked Trout with Mascarpone Scrambled Eggs

When time is not an issue why not sit down and enjoy this indulgent weekend breakfast dish?

Servings: 4

Prep Time: 7mins

Cooking Time: 6min

Total Time: 13mins

Ingredients:

- 4 medium eggs
- ¾ cup mascarpone
- Sea salt
- Cracked black pepper
- 4 tsp unsalted butter
- 8 thin slices sourdough toast
- 6 ounces smoked trout (flaked)
- Mixed herb seasoning

Directions:

1. Add the eggs, mascarpone, sea salt, and black pepper to a large mixing bowl, and whisk to combine.

2. In a frying pan, over moderate heat, melt the butter

3. Add the egg mixture to the pan and cook, without stirring, for 40 seconds, or until the mixture is beginning to firm.

4. Gently scramble, using a wooden spoon, until just cooked.

5. Spoon the scrambled eggs over the toast, along with the flaked trout. Scatter with mixed herbs, and season to taste.

Southern Sausage Gravy

This classic Southern breakfast is the best way to start the day; creamy gravy served over fluffy biscuits.

Servings: 8

Prep Time: 3mins

Cooking Time: 7mins

Total Time: 10mins

Ingredients:

- 1 pound pork sausage
- ¼ cup all-purpose flour
- 2 cups whole milk
- Sea salt and black pepper
- Hot buttermilk biscuits

Directions:

1. Warm a cast iron skillet over moderate heat.

2. Add the sausage to the skillet, breaking it into chunks using a wooden spoon or spatula.

3. Cook until the crumbled sausage meat is browned through.

4. Add the flour and continue cooking until dissolved, for 60 minutes.

5. Pour in the milk, while stirring.

6. Cook, while frequently whisking, until the gravy is bubbly and beginning to thicken.

7. Season with sea salt and black pepper.

8. Serve with the hot biscuits.

Spinach and Egg Frittata

A protein-packed hot cooked breakfast is just what the doctor ordered.

Servings: 1-2

Prep Time: 4mins

Cooking Time: 8mins

Total Time: 12mins

Ingredients:

- 1-2 cups frozen spinach
- 1 small shallot (minced)
- 2 tbsp. butter
- Salt and black pepper
- 2 medium eggs (beaten)

Directions:

1. Defrost the spinach in a microwave for 60 seconds.

2. In the meantime, and while the spinach defrosts, sauté the shallots in a cast iron skillet in butter, over moderate heat.

3. Remove the spinach from the microwave, and squeeze it dry.

4. Add a dash of salt and pepper to the beaten eggs.

5. Transfer the spinach to the skillet, along with the eggs and stir thoroughly until the shallots are incorporated.

6. Lower the heat to moderate to low and allow the frittata to set before flipping and cooking the other side.

7. When sufficiently cooked through, serve.

Sweet and Savory

Cinnamon French Toast and Pancetta Casserole

your next long, lazy weekend breakfast, try this sweet and savory breakfast recipe.

Servings: 4-6

Prep Time: 15mins

Cooking Time: 50mins

Total Time: 9hours 5mins

Ingredients:

- Butter (for greasing)
- ¼ pound pancetta (finely chopped))
- 8 ounces Italian ricotta
- 1 tbsp. + ½ tsp cinnamon
- 1½ tsp vanilla essence
- ¼ cup dark brown sugar
- 5 eggs
- ½ cup half & half
- 1 small ciabatta loaf (thinly sliced)
- 2 tbsp. turbinado sugar

Directions:

1. First, lightly grease a square 8" baking dish and set to one side.

2. Heat a frying pan over moderate heat and cook the pancetta for 5-7 minutes, until cooked through and crisp. Take the pan off the heat and set to one side to cool.

3. In a bowl, combine the ricotta cheese, along with 1½ tsp of cinnamon, followed by the vanilla essence and dark brown sugar.

4. In a clean mixing bowl whisk together the eggs, along with the half & half, and 2 tsp of cinnamon.

5. Use some of the sliced bread to make an even layer in the base of the baking dish.

6. Next, evenly spread the cheese mixture over the ciabatta.

7. Sprinkle over the cooled pancetta and lay the remaining slices of bread on top of the pancetta.

8. Pour the liquid mixture carefully over the bread, and cover with a sheet of plastic wrap. Transfer to the fridge to chill, overnight.

9. Allow the casserole to rest at room temperature for half an hour.

10. Scatter with the turbinado sugar.

11. Preheat the main oven to 350 degrees F and bake in the oven for just over 35 minutes or until the liquid is firmly set. Serve.

Fennel Maple Bacon

A sophisticated and classy addition to any breakfast spread.

Portions: 4

Prep Time: 10mins

Cooking Time: 25mins

Total Time: 35mins

Ingredients:

- 3 tbsp. maple syrup
- 1 tbsp. brown sugar
- 12 rashers bacon (thick-cut)
- 2 tsp crushed fennel seeds
- Black pepper (freshly ground)

Directions:

1. Preheat the main oven to 375 degrees F and line a baking sheet with aluminum foil. Set a wire rack on the baking sheet. Set aside for a moment.

2. Whisk together the maple syrup and sugar, in a small jug.

3. Arrange the rashers of bacon on the wire rack. Brush the maple mixture evenly over the bacon. Sprinkle with crushed fennel seeds and black pepper.

4. Place in the oven and bake until crispy, just over 20 minutes.

5. Serve hot.

Fried Banana Bacon Breakfast Sandwiches

A salty sweet marriage of crispy bacon and ripe banana sandwiched together in raisin cinnamon muffins and slathered with maple mascarpone.

Portions: 2-4

Prep Time: 10mins

Cooking Time: 5mins

Total Time: 15mins

Ingredients:

- 4 rashers bacon (thick-cut)
- 1 tbsp. canola oil
- 1 underripe medium banana (peeled, sliced ½" thick)
- 1 tbsp. organic honey
- 1 tbsp. water
- ¼ tsp cinnamon
- ½ cup mascarpone cheese
- 1 tbsp. maple syrup
- 2 raisin cinnamon English muffins (halved, toasted)

Directions:

1. Fry the bacon until crispy and set aside on a kitchen paper lined dish.

2. In a skillet, heat the oil over moderately high heat, while swirling.

3. When hot, add the sliced banana to the skillet. Cook for 60 seconds before flipping the banana slices and cooking for another 60 seconds. Take the pan off the heat. Set to one side for a moment.

4. Whisk together the honey and water. Pour the honey mixture over the banana in the skillet. Toss to coat the banana in the liquid.

5. Sprinkle with the cinnamon.

6. Whip up the mascarpone cheese and whisk in the maple syrup.

7. Spread the mascarpone cheese equally over the toasted muffin halves. Top each muffin half with an equal amount of caramelized banana and one rasher of bacon.

Peach and Bacon Omelet

How do you like your eggs in the morning? We like ours with peaches and bacon. Make this Omega 3 rich breakfast, and you won't have any trouble getting your family to the breakfast table.

Servings: 2-3

Prep Time: 15mins

Cooking Time: 10mins

Total Time: 25mins

Ingredients:

- 1 cup peaches (peeled, pitted, sliced)
- 2 tbsp. freshly squeezed lemon juice
- 4 slices bacon
- 2 tbsp. cold water
- 6 medium eggs
- 1 tsp fresh chives (chopped)
- ¼ tsp salt
- 1 tbsp. white sugar
- ⅛ tsp ground black pepper
- 1 pinch paprika

Directions:

1. In a bowl, combine the peach slices with the freshly squeezed lemon juice and combine. Set to one side.

2. In a large frying pan or skillet, over moderate to high heat, fry the bacon until crispy. Transfer the bacon to a kitchen paper lined plate. Drain the skillet but leave 1 tbsp. of bacon fat in the skillet.

3. When the bacon is sufficiently cool; crumble.

4. In a mixing bowl, combine the crumbled bacon along with the cold water, eggs, chopped chives, salt, white sugar and ground pepper.

5. Over a moderate to high heat, reheat the bacon fat.

6. As soon as the fat is hot, pour the egg mixture into the frying pan.

7. Arrange the slices of peaches on top of the batter, cover the pan with a lid, and over moderate heat, cook for 60 seconds.

8. Remove the lid and continue to cook until set.

9. Scatter with paprika and serve.

Peaches and Cream Breakfast Cake with Cottage Cheese

A sweet and fluffy breakfast cake that is healthy yet delicious, and packed with protein thanks to the cottage cheese.

Portions: 8

Prep Time: 10mins

Cooking Time: 50mins

Total Time: 1hour 30mins

Ingredients:

- Butter (for greasing)
- ½ cup + 1 tbsp. granulated sugar
- 3 medium eggs
- 1 cup low-fat cottage cheese
- 6 tbsp. salted butter (melted)
- 1 tsp vanilla essence
- 1 cup 0% plain Greek yogurt
- ¾ cup all-purpose flour
- 1½ tsp baking powder
- ½ tsp kosher salt
- 1½ cups fresh peaches (pitted, sliced)

Directions:

1. Preheat the main oven to 350 degrees F and grease an 8" round springform tin.

2. Beat together the sugar and eggs, until creamy. Whisk in the cottage cheese, melted butter, vanilla, and yogurt, until combined.

3. Beat in the flour, baking powder, and salt, until just incorporated.

4. Pour the batter into the tin and arrange the sliced peaches on top of the batter.

5. Place in the oven and bake for approximately 50 minutes, until set in the center.

6. Allow the cooked cake to rest at room temperature for half an hour to become firm.

7. Slice and serve while still warm.

Pear and Bacon Grilled Cheese Sandwich

Breakfast is considered to be the most important meal of the day, so make it count!

Servings: 2

Prep Time: 7mins

Cooking Time: 7mins

Total Time: 14mins

Ingredients:

- 4 slices sourdough
- 4 slices Cheddar cheese
- 1 firm, ripe pear (peeled, cored, halved lengthwise, cut into 4)
- 4 slices cooked bacon
- 2 tbsp. butter (softened)

Directions:

1. Arrange 2 slices of sourdough bread on a clean, work surface.

2. Top each slice with a piece of Cheddar cheese.

3. Arrange 2 pear slices on top of the cheese along with 2 slices of cooked bacon, and then top with a second slice of Cheddar cheese.

4. Place a slice of sourdough bread on the top and butter each top slice of bread with 1 tablespoon of butter.

5. Preheat a large frying pan or skillet.

6. Place the sandwiches buttered side facing down in the hot skillet.

7. Next, with the remaining butter, butter the top side of each sandwich and cook until browned, flip over and brown on the other side.

8. Cut each of the sandwiches in half and serve.

Pomegranate and Avocado Superfood Toast

This sweet and savory breakfast is a triple threat; nutritious, delicious, and super quick to whip up!

Portions: 1

Prep Time: 10mins

Cooking Time: 5mins

Total Time: 15mins

Ingredients:

- 1 small ripe avocado (peeled, pitted, mashed)
- Freshly squeezed juice from ½ a medium lime
- 2 tbsp. fresh coriander (chopped)
- 1 tbsp. virgin olive oil
- Pinch sea salt flakes
- 1 thick cut slice wholegrain bread (toasted)
- 1 tbsp. hemp seeds
- 2 tbsp. fresh pomegranate arils
- Organic honey

Directions:

1. Mash together the avocado, lime juice, coriander, olive oil, and a pinch of sea salt. Spread the mixture onto the toasted bread while still hot.

2. Scatter with hemp seeds, pomegranate arils, and finish with a drizzle of honey and pinch of sea salt flakes.

Raspberry Brie Grilled Cheese

If you haven't had the pleasure of enjoying cheese with sweet fruity jam, then you'll be blown away by this simple yet utterly yummy grownup grilled cheese.

Portions: 4

Prep Time: 10mins

Cooking Time: 15mins

Total Time: 25mins

Ingredients:

- ⅓ cup organic raspberry jam
- 8 slices thick cut wholegrain crusty bread
- 12 ounce French Brie (sliced)
- 3 tbsp. salted butter (melted)

Directions:

1. Generously spread the jam evenly over four of the slices of bread. Arrange the sliced Brie on top of the jam covered slices. Sandwich the remaining four slices on top, to make four sandwiches in total.

2. Brush the melted butter over both sides of every sandwich.

3. In a skillet over moderately high heat, cook each sandwich, individually flipping when golden, and continuing to cook until the cheese melts.

4. Slice each sandwich in half and serve.

Strawberry Chili Jam Breakfast Sandwich

If you are looking for a sweet yet savory breakfast to help get your out of bed, then this is the one!

Servings: 1

Prep Time: 5mins

Cooking Time: 25mins

Total Time: 30mins

Ingredients:

- ½ tbsp. coconut oil
- 1 medium shallot (minced)
- 1½ cups strawberries (coarsely chopped)
- 2 tbsp. chili peppers (thinly sliced)
- 2 tbsp. apple cider vinegar
- 1 tbsp. coconut sugar
- 2-3 slices bread (toasted)
- 4 slices cooked bacon (crispy)
- 1 medium egg (fried)

Directions:

1. Over moderate heat, add the coconut oil to a small pan.

2. When sufficiently hot, add the minced shallots and fry for 60 seconds until fragrant and softened.

3. Next, add the chopped strawberries, along with the chili peppers, apple cider vinegar, and coconut sugar. Stir well to incorporate and bring to boil.

4. As soon as the mixture is boiling, reduce the heat to low and gently simmer, occasionally stirring so that the strawberries thicken and reduce, this will take around 20-25 minutes. Remove the pan from the heat and set to one side to cool.

5. Next, assemble the sandwich: Spoon the jam onto the hot toasted bread, place the bacon on top of the chili jam and finish with the fried egg.

6. Store any leftover jam in an airtight, resealable container in the fridge for up to 14 days.

Zucchini and Pineapple Bread

Wake up to this special occasion breakfast bread. When toast simply isn't good enough!

Servings: 6-8

Prep Time: 10mins

Cooking Time: 1hour

Total Time: 1hour 40mins

Ingredients:

- Canola oil (for greasing)
- 2 cups sugar
- 3 large eggs
- 2 cups zucchini (shredded)
- 1 cup vegetable oil
- 2 tbsp. vanilla extract
- 3 cups all-purpose flour
- 1 tsp baking powder
- 1 tsp baking soda
- 1 tsp iodized salt
- 1 cup pineapple (crushed)
- 1 cup walnuts (roughly chopped)
- Jelly, jam or butter (for serving)

Directions:

1. Preheat the main oven to 350 degrees F. Grease 2 (8x4") loaf pans with canola oil.

2. In a large mixing bowl, and using an electric mixer on moderate speed, beat the sugar along with the eggs, for 2-3 minutes, or until light and creamy.

3. Next, add the shredded zucchini, olive oil, and vanilla extract and continue beating for a couple more minutes.

4. In another mixing bowl, combine the all-purpose flour with the baking powder and soda, and salt.

5. Stir the dry mixture carefully into the egg mixture.

6. Gradually, add the pineapple and fold in, along with the chopped walnuts.

7. Evenly divide the mixture between the prepared loaf pans.

8. Bake for approximately an hour, until set in the center.

9. Allow the bread to cool in the loaf pans for half an hour.

10. Remove from the pans and place on wire baking racks until totally cool.

11. Serve toasted and warm with jelly, jam or butter.

About the Author

Martha is a chef and a cookbook author. She has had a love of all things culinary since she was old enough to help in the kitchen, and hasn't wanted to leave the kitchen since. She was born and raised in Illinois, and grew up on a farm, where she acquired her love for fresh, delicious foods. She learned many of her culinary abilities from her mother; most importantly, the need to cook with fresh, homegrown ingredients if at all possible, and how to create an amazing recipe that everyone wants. This gave her the perfect way to share her skill with the world; writing cookbooks to spread the message that fresh, healthy food really can, and does, taste delicious. Now that she is a mother, it is more important than ever to make sure that healthy food is available to the next generation. She hopes to become a household name in cookbooks for her delicious recipes, and healthy outlook.

Martha is now living in California with her high school sweetheart, and now husband, John, as well as their infant daughter Isabel, and two dogs; Daisy and Sandy. She is a stay at home mom, who is very much looking forward to expanding their family in the next few years to give their daughter some siblings. She enjoys cooking with, and for, her family and friends, and is waiting impatiently for the day she can start cooking with her daughter.

Author's Afterthoughts

Thanks ever so much to each of my cherished readers for investing the time to read this book!

I know you could have picked from many other books but you chose this one. So a big thanks for downloading this book and reading all the way to the end.

If you enjoyed this book or received value from it, I'd like to ask you for a favor. Please take a few minutes to post an honest and heartfelt review on Amazon.com. Your support does make a difference and helps to benefit other people.

Thanks!

Martha Stephenson

Made in the USA
Middletown, DE
05 December 2018